DISEASES

eXtreme FACTS

BY ROBIN TWIDDY

©2019
The Secret Book Company
King's Lynn
Norfolk PE30 4LS

ISBN: 978-1-912502-85-1

All rights reserved
Printed in Malaysia

Written by:
Robin Twiddy
Edited by:
Madeline Tyler
Designed by:
Jasmine Pointer

A catalogue record for this book
is available from the British Library.

All facts, statistics, web addresses and URLs in this book were verified as valid and accurate at time of writing. No responsibility for any changes to external websites or references can be accepted by either the author or publisher.

PHOTO CREDITS

Front cover – VikiVector, VectorGoddess, Markovka, Telnov Oleksii, svtdesign, Alona Syplyak, A7880S, Andrew Rybalk0, Smart Design, Maksim M Suz7, ghrzuzudu , Artit Fongfung, AVA Bitter, Creative Mood, Rvector. 4 – Rvector, Lorelyn Medina, Roman Beresnev. 5 – RedlineVector, Macrovector. 6–7 – NotionPic, Good_Stock, VikiVector, Olga Bolbot, Marnikus, notkoo, CoCoArt_Ua, Dukesn, Nemanja Cosovic, ksanask.art. 8 – vectorpouch, NotionPic, iana kauri, lady-luck. 9 – moj0j0, AlexHliv. 10 – barkarola, illpos, Darin8005. 11 – vladwel, jkcDesign, Faber14. 12 – Alex Kednert, Achiichiii, Stocklifemax, fullvector. 13 – SimpleThings, solar22, Sapann Design. 14 – Mountain Brothers, Jemastock, Humdan, MicroOne. 15 – asantosg, peiyang, Nina Puankova, Leremy. 16 – stickerama, Glinskaja Olga. 17 – art4all, Jiw Ingka, Tatyana Pogorelova, Nadia Snopek. 18 – MatiasDelCarmine, Irina Strelnikova, NotionPic, Here.19 – Artit Fongfung, WhiteDragon, svtdesign, Eroshka. 20 – Top Vector Studio, Lemberg Vector studio, svtdesign, MSSA. 21 – ankomando, tynyuk, Inspiring, Antonov Maxim. 22 – KittyVector, Lorelyn Medina, JaynaKubat, tynyuk, Pavel Kukol. 23 – tynyuk, MuchMania, Nutkins J, Febry Octopus. Images are courtesy of Shutterstock.com. With thanks to Getty Images, Thinkstock Photo and iStockphoto.

CONTENTS

Words that look like <u>this</u> can be found in the glossary on page 24.

EXTREMELY UNLIKELY CAUSES

Before doctors and scientists helped us to understand that diseases are caused by <u>bacteria</u> and <u>genetics</u>, people had some very strange ideas about what did cause them.

People once believed that Brussels sprouts contained **demons**. They thought that eating them would make you fart and become ill.

In Eastern Europe, **people** used to believe that people with tuberculosis were being visited by **vampires** in the night and having their life energy sucked out of them.

When trains were first introduced in England, many people believed that travelling by train could cause 'railway madness'.

Since the 4th century <u>BC</u> until the 19th century <u>AD</u>, lots of medicine was based on the four humours and the idea that people would become ill if the humours were out of balance.

The four humours are:

Phlegm

Black <u>bile</u>

Yellow bile

Blood

The ancient Maya believed that illness and disease was caused by breaking the laws of nature and the laws of their <u>society</u>.

The ancient Egyptians believed that <u>spirits</u> blocked channels in the body that energy should flow through, and this caused disease.

EXTREMELY UNLIKELY CURES

Along with unlikely causes, there were also some unlikely cures.

If a person's humours were out of balance, then people believed bloodletting could be a cure.

The ancient Romans believed that drinking the blood of a gladiator could cure epilepsy.

One popular way of bloodletting was using leeches. These are small blood-sucking creatures that are placed on the skin.

Trepanation is the practice of drilling holes in the skull. It was used for thousands of years to treat head injuries and brain diseases. Some people think it was done to let spirits out of the head.

The ancient Egyptians **believed that blood from bats could cure blindness.**

One <u>medieval</u> cure for the common cold (that didn't work) was to drink human blood. **The Germans and the French both had recipes for turning blood into marmalade.**

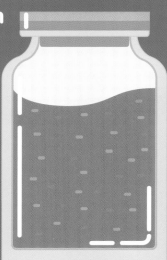

If you needed blood for medicine, or to make marmalade, you could buy some at a public <u>execution</u> in the 17th century.

The ancient Maya used herbs to treat diseases. **Different coloured herbs were used for different things.**
- **Red herbs: rashes**
- **Yellow herbs: diseases**

THE BLACK DEATH

The Black Death, also known as the Great Plague, was a disease that spread across Europe between AD 1347 and AD 1351.

Plague is caused by bacteria called Y. pestis. There are three different types of plague: bubonic, septicaemic and pneumonic. **Each version has its own** <u>symptoms</u>.

A type of flea that lives on black rats carried the bacteria. Historians believe that it was bites from these fleas that started the plague.

Some suggested cures for the plague included:
- **Rubbing onions or chopped up snake on the boils**
- **Sitting in a sewer**
- **Drinking vinegar**

Plague doctors were hired by towns and cities to treat people suffering from the plague.

Plague doctors are well known for their uniform of long leather robes, a top hat and a beak-shaped mask. The mask was filled with dried flowers and other sweet-smelling things.

The most famous plague doctor was Nostradamus. He was French and lived around 500 years ago.

Around 25 million people died from the Black Death in Europe.

SPANISH INFLUENZA

Spanish influenza, or Spanish flu, killed between 50 million and 100 million people between 1918 and 1919.

The flu spread during World War I (WWI). Neither side wanted the other to know that they were sick, so they kept it secret.

The name Spanish influenza was given to the disease when it reached Spain. Spain didn't take a side in the war, so it did not need to keep the disease secret.

WWI made it much easier for the flu to spread because of the poor living conditions of the soldiers, and the movement of both soldiers and <u>civilians</u>.

When the Spanish flu was at its worst, you could be fined for not covering your mouth **when you coughed, and even be arrested for shaking hands with someone.**

Spanish flu killed more people than either WWI or the Black Death.

Only one place on Earth was not affected by Spanish flu – a <u>remote</u> island called Marajo in Brazil.

LEPROSY

Leprosy is a disease that affects the nerves in a person's skin.

Each year, around 100 people in the US are diagnosed with leprosy.

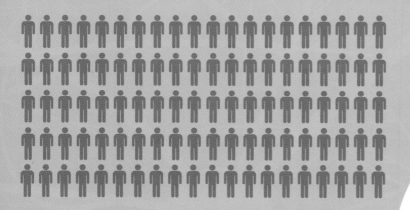

Leprosy symptoms can take as long as 20 years to appear.

Leprosy can be cured with today's modern medicine.

It is a myth that leprosy causes fingers, toes, arms or legs to fall off.

People with leprosy used to be sent to live in 'leper colonies', usually alone on islands.

Today over nine out of ten people are immune to leprosy.

The modern name for leprosy is Hansen's disease.

POLIO

Polio is a very serious disease that can cause <u>paralysis</u> and even death.

Polio has no cure, but it can be <u>prevented</u> with <u>vaccinations</u>.

1 in 200 infections of polio leads to paralysis.

Polio can cause death if the breathing muscles are paralysed.

Thanks to the use of vaccines, there have been no cases of polio beginning in the US since 1979.

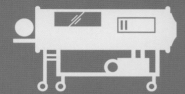

The iron lung was invented to help people with paralysed breathing muscles breathe.

Franklin D. Roosevelt, the 32nd president of the US, had polio. He started a charity that helped to create the first successful polio vaccine.

Global efforts to <u>eradicate</u> polio have led to a 99.9 percent (%) drop in cases around the world.

EXTREMELY WEIRD DISEASES

Some diseases can have really weird symptoms.

There is a rare disease that leaves some people with an allergy to water. People with the allergy are even allergic to their own sweat.

There is a disease called fatal familial insomnia and one of its main symptoms is not being able to sleep.

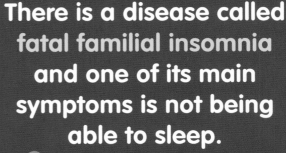

Hypertrichosis is a rare genetic disease that causes extra hair to grow in places people don't normally have a lot of hair. It is sometimes known as werewolf syndrome.

A rare disease, known as 'tree-man disease' or EV, causes bark-like growths on the hands, feet and other parts of the body.

Another very rare disease causes muscles and <u>tendons</u> to gradually be replaced with bone, turning the person into a living statue.

Necrotising fasciitis is sometimes called the 'flesh-eating' bacteria. The bacteria don't actually eat flesh, but they do release <u>toxins</u> that damage the body.

Laughing death was a disease where the victim would laugh loudly, cross their eyes and then fall down dead. The disease was said to be caught by eating dead bodies at funerals.

PEOPLE WHO FOUGHT DISEASES

Hippocrates was an ancient Greek doctor. Many people say that he was the greatest doctor of his time. Doctors still take the Hippocratic Oath – a promise to do no harm to anybody.

Metrodora was the first woman to write a medical book. She wrote it somewhere between AD 200 and AD 400.

Edward Jenner created the first vaccine in 1796. Thanks to his work, many diseases are now under control and some, such as smallpox, have even been eradicated.

Louis Pasteur introduced the world to the germ theory of disease. This is the theory that diseases are caused by <u>microorganisms</u>.

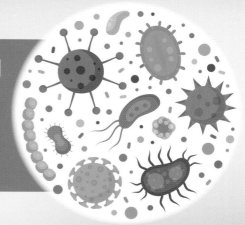

Joseph Lister invented <u>antiseptic</u> medicine. He was the first to say that bacteria should never enter a wound, especially in surgery.

Florence Nightingale is famous for starting one of the first professional schools for nursing. She made huge changes to medicine. She was also known as the 'Lady with the Lamp'.

Alexander Fleming discovered penicillin in 1928. It is one of the most widely used <u>antibiotics</u> for fighting disease.

FIGHTING DISEASES

Using vaccines and a lot of teamwork, medical professionals have managed to eradicate smallpox worldwide.

Just like animals, viruses can evolve. When they do, it can make it harder for our medicine and bodies to fight them.

The x-ray scanner is an important piece of equipment for fighting disease, but did you know that it was discovered by accident?

Healthy living is one of the best ways to prevent diseases.

The World Health Organization suggests that different age groups need different amounts of physical activity to stay healthy and fight off disease.

Children aged 5–17 years should do about an hour of physical activity a day.

Adults aged 18–64 years should do at least 150 minutes of physical activity a week.

Adults aged 65 years and older should do 150 minutes of gentle physical activity a week.

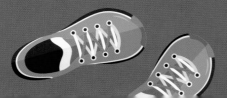

ANIMAL DISEASES

Chimpanzees can catch Ebola, a disease mostly thought of as a human disease.

Rabies is a disease that any warm-blooded animal can catch. It is spread through the saliva of the diseased animal.

Mad cow disease affects the brain and nerves of cows. Humans can catch a human version of the disease if they eat the brain or nerves of a diseased cow.

If a pet loses the use of its legs to a disease, they can now have an animal wheelchair fitted to help them get around.

The first veterinary school was built in France in **1761**.

By studying animals with similar diseases to ones that humans catch, scientists have learnt how to treat those diseases.

Because livestock, such as cows and sheep, live close together in herds or flocks, diseases can spread quickly.

Malaria is a disease caused by a <u>parasite</u> carried by **mosquitoes.** Even though the mosquitoes carry the parasite, they don't suffer from the disease.

GLOSSARY

AD — after the birth of Jesus, which is used as the starting point for many calendars around the world
antibiotics — substances used to destroy or prevent the growth of bacteria
antiseptic — preventing the growth of bacteria
bacteria — tiny living things, which are too small to see, that can cause diseases
BC — meaning 'before Christ', this is used to mark dates that occurred before the starting year of most calendars
bile — a yellow or dark-green fluid in the stomach that helps break down food
bloodletting — removing blood from the body
civilians — people who are not in the military or armed forces
epilepsy — a brain condition that causes seizures (bursts of electrical activity in the brain that temporarily affect how it works)
eradicate — to completely remove
evolve — to change and develop over time
execution — the carrying out of a death sentence
genetics — the science of how characteristics are passed from parent to offspring
gladiator — a warrior in ancient Rome who fought others to entertain an audience
immune — protected from a disease
medieval — the period of time between the 5th and the 15th century
microorganisms — tiny organisms, such as bacteria, that are too small to be seen with the naked eye
paralysis — loss of feeling in a body part or not being able to move it
parasite — a living thing that lives on or in another living thing
prevented — stopped something from happening
remote — far away from people
society — a collection of people living together at a certain time
spirits — beings that are not part of this world, such as a ghost or devil
symptoms — things that happen in the body suggesting that there is a disease or disorder
tendons — the things that connect muscles with bones or other body parts
toxins — poisonous substances produced by plants or animals
vaccinations — treatments that produce immunity against a disease

INDEX